Flowers and Floral

COLORING BOOK

Stress Relieving Patterns
Adult Coloring Books

COLOR TEST PAGE

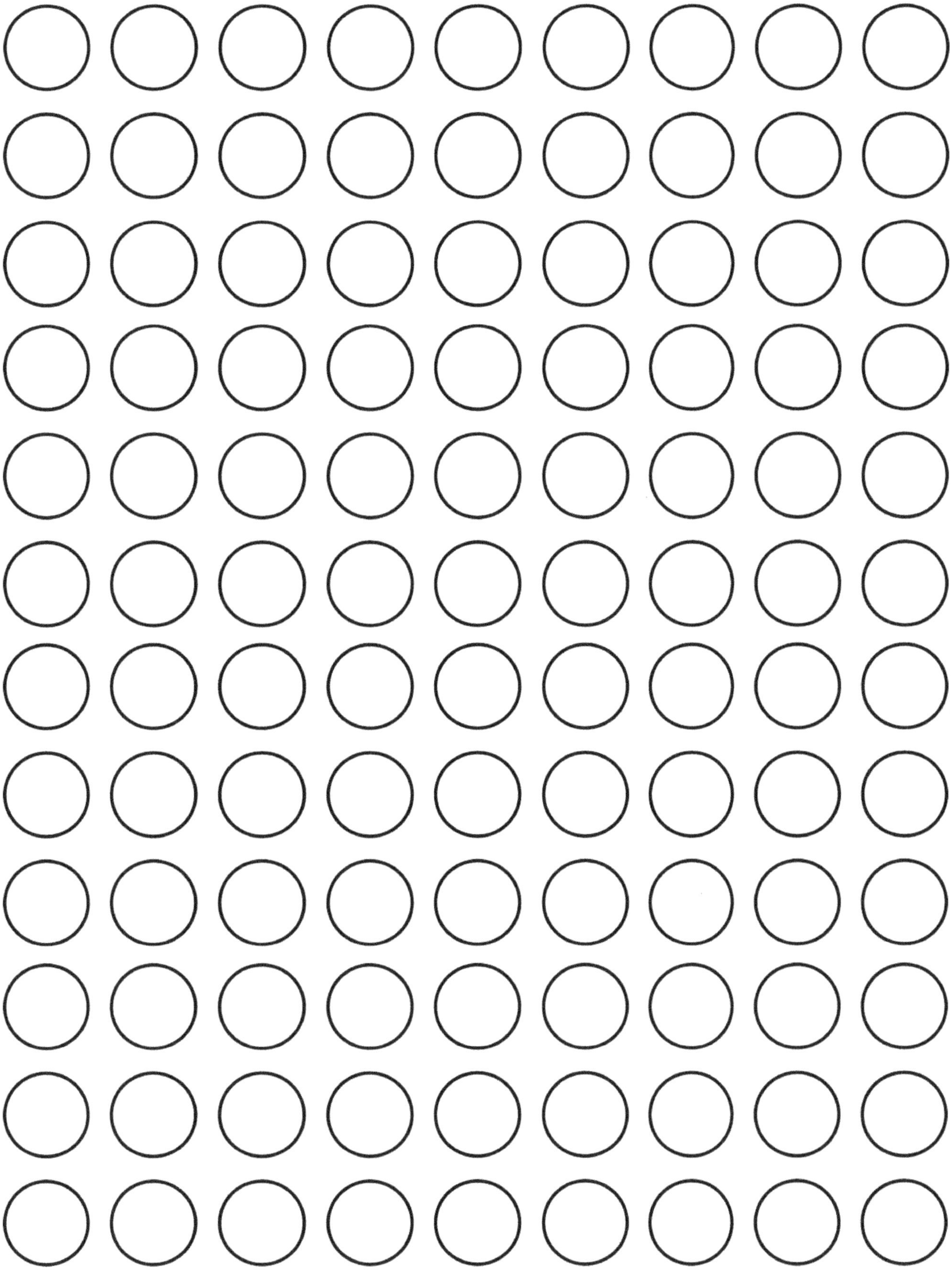

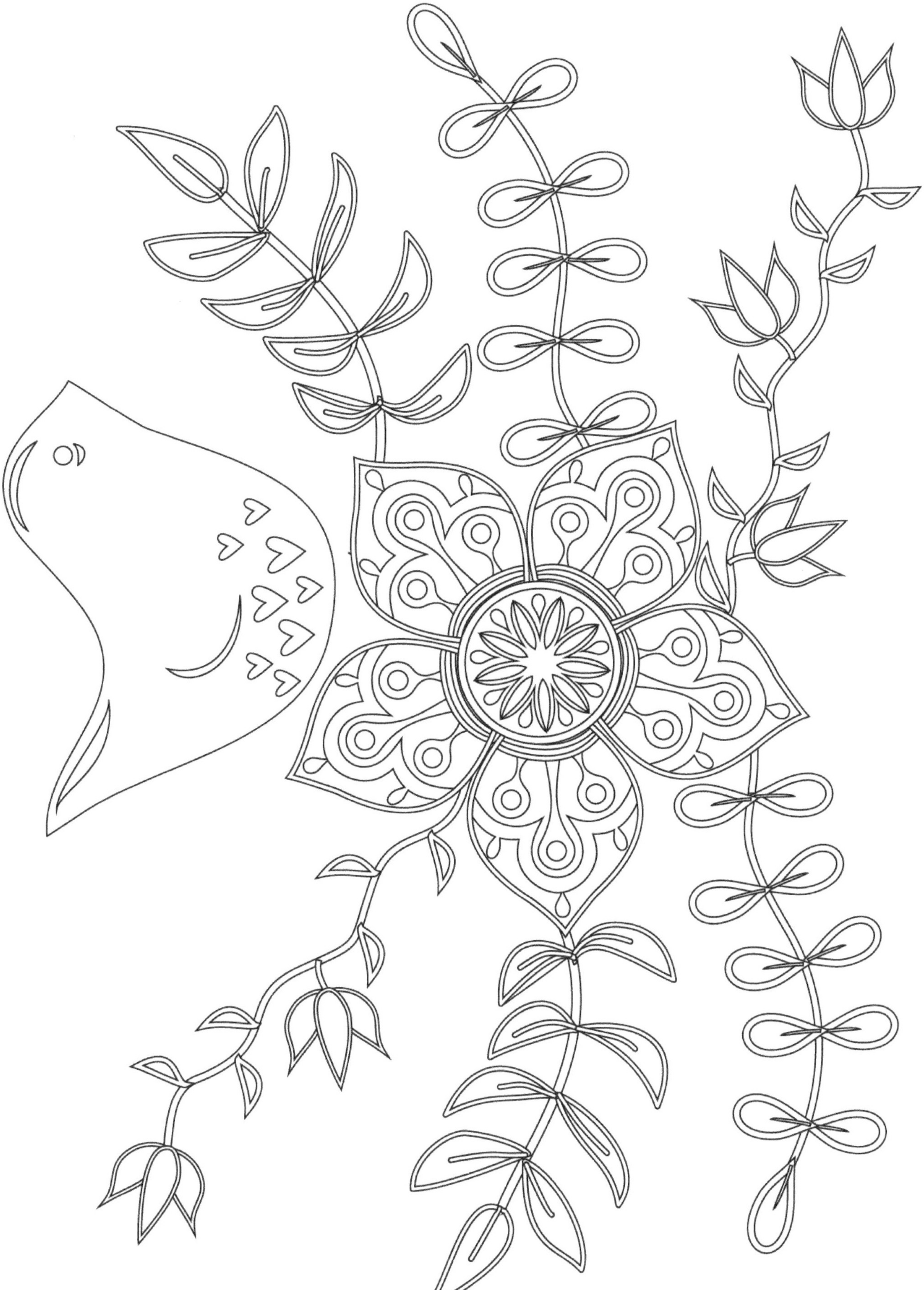

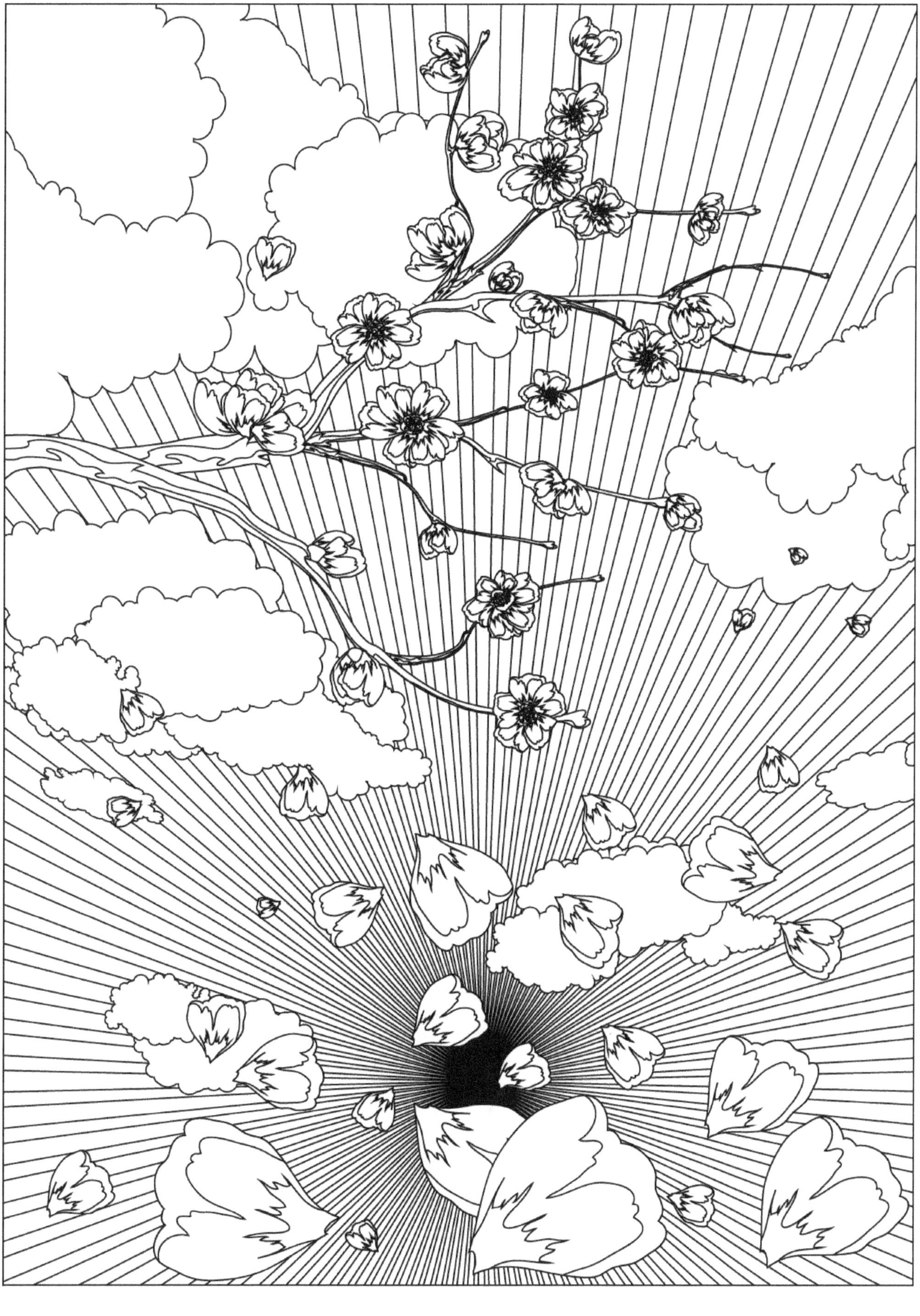

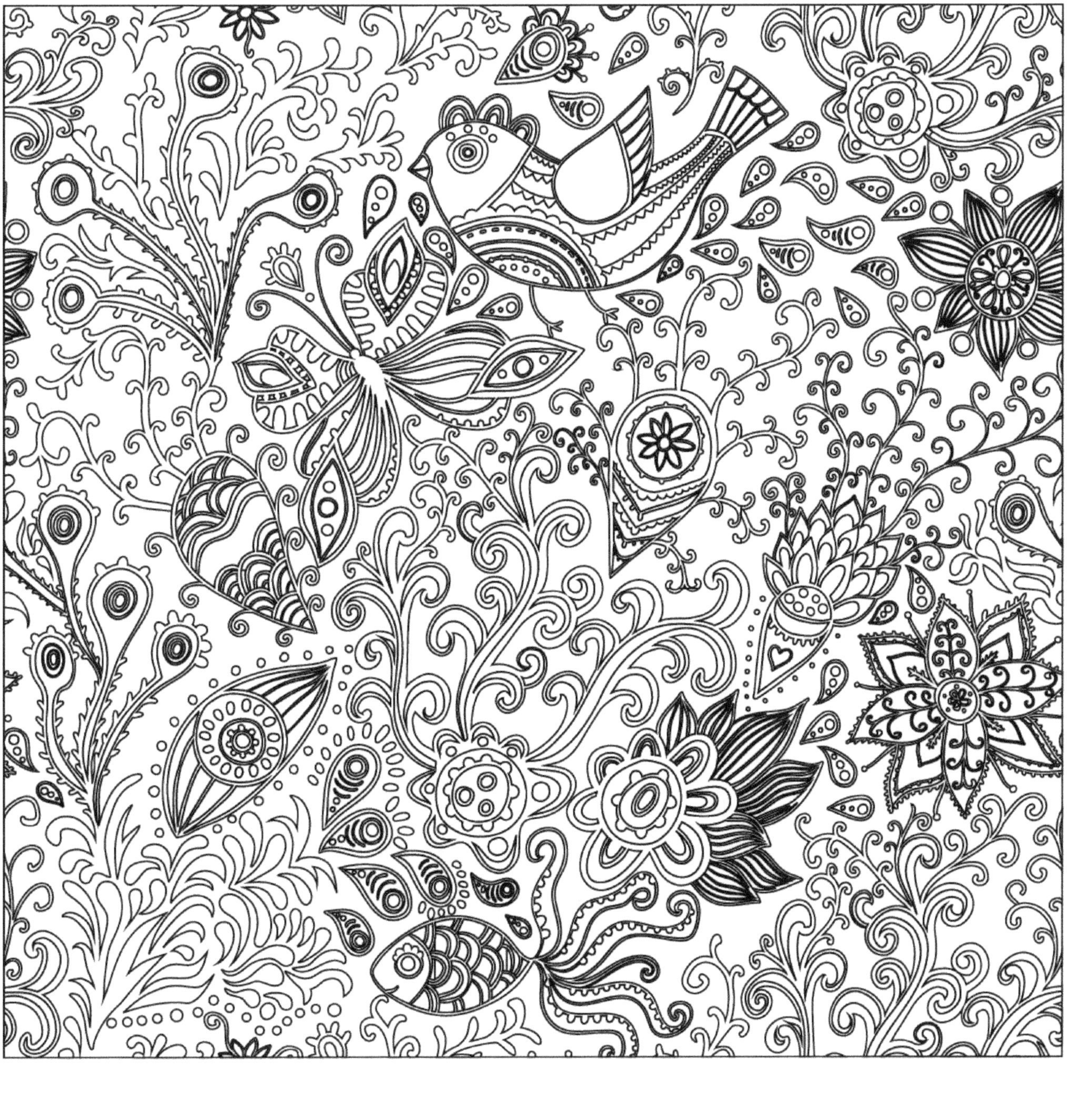

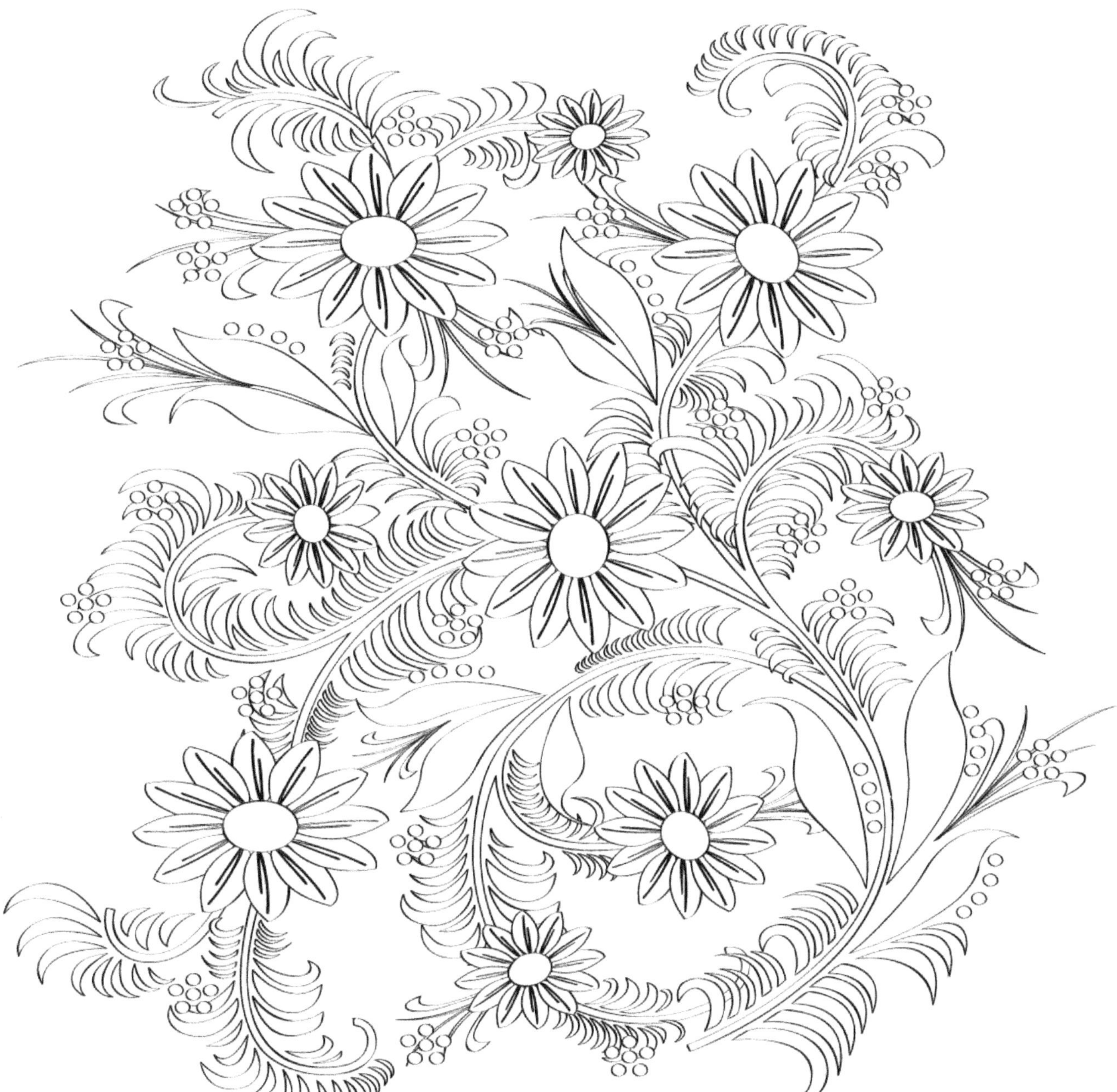

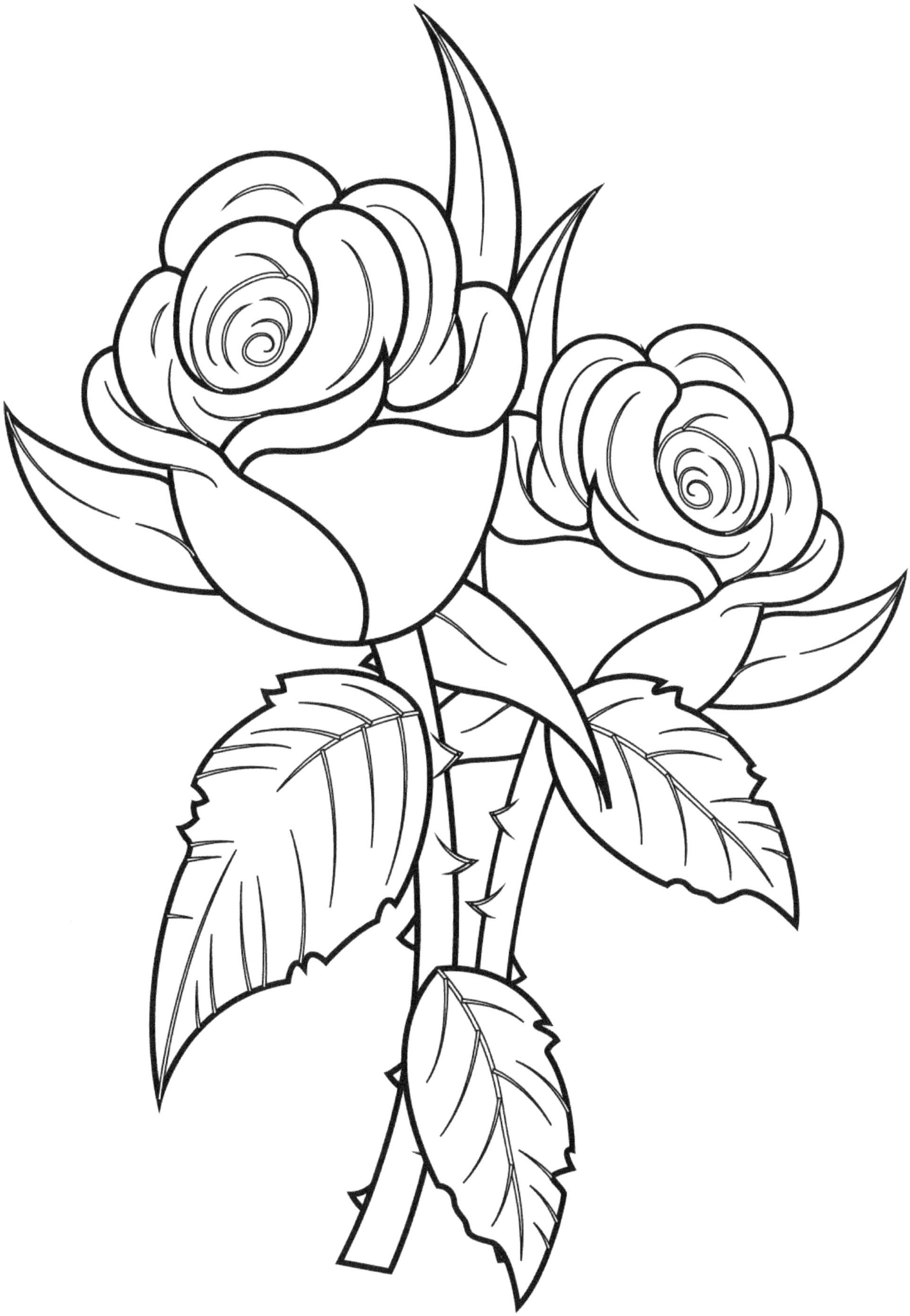

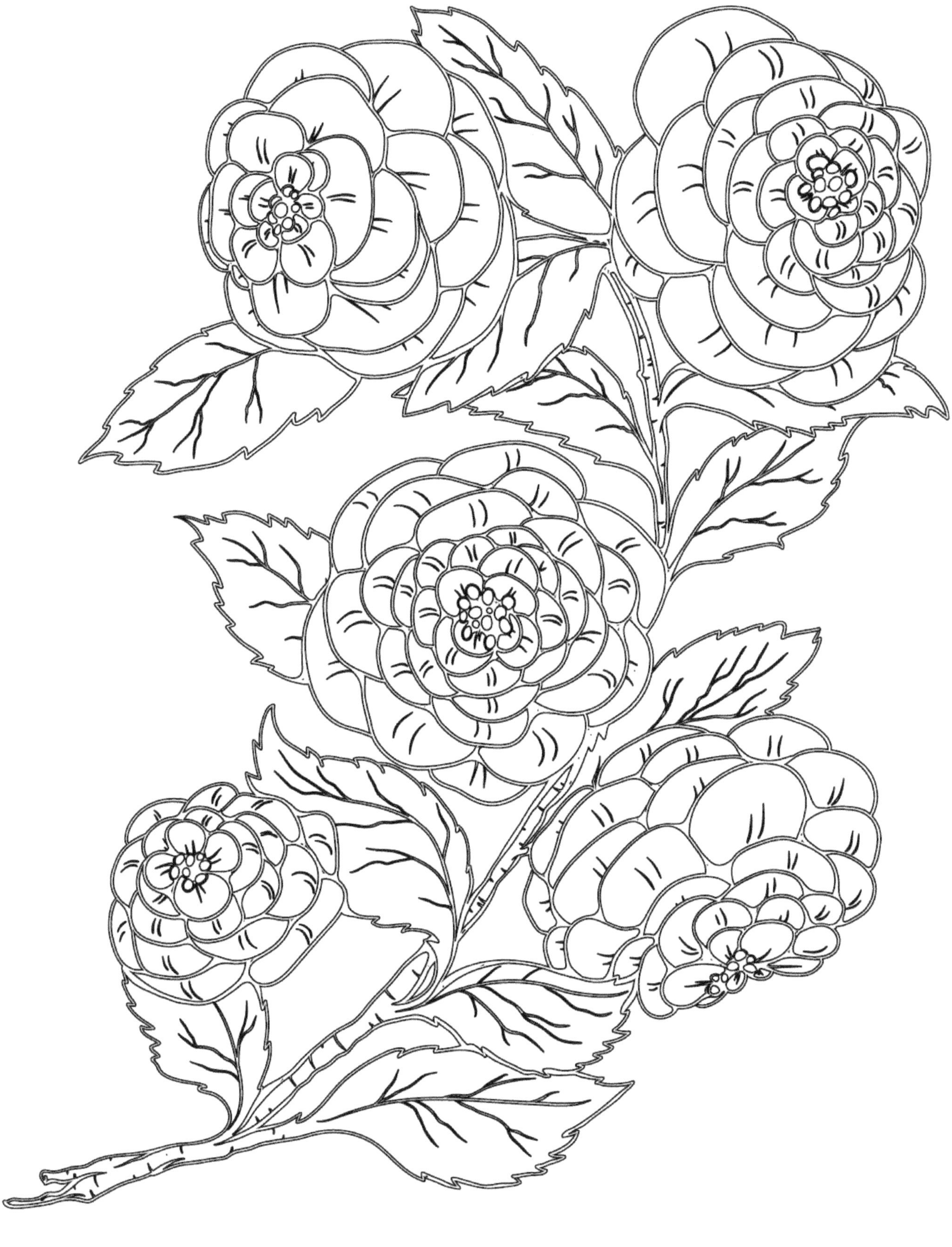

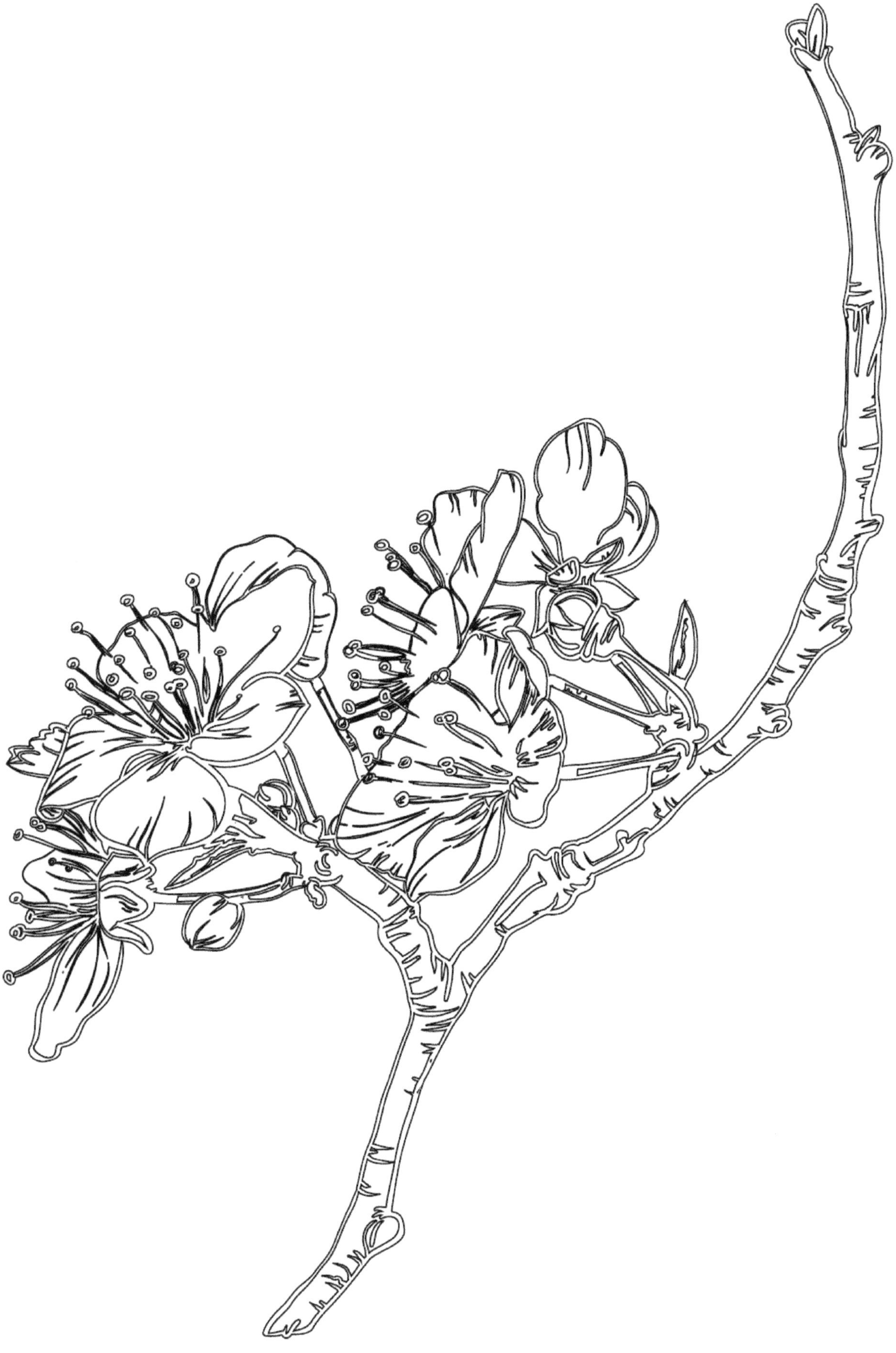

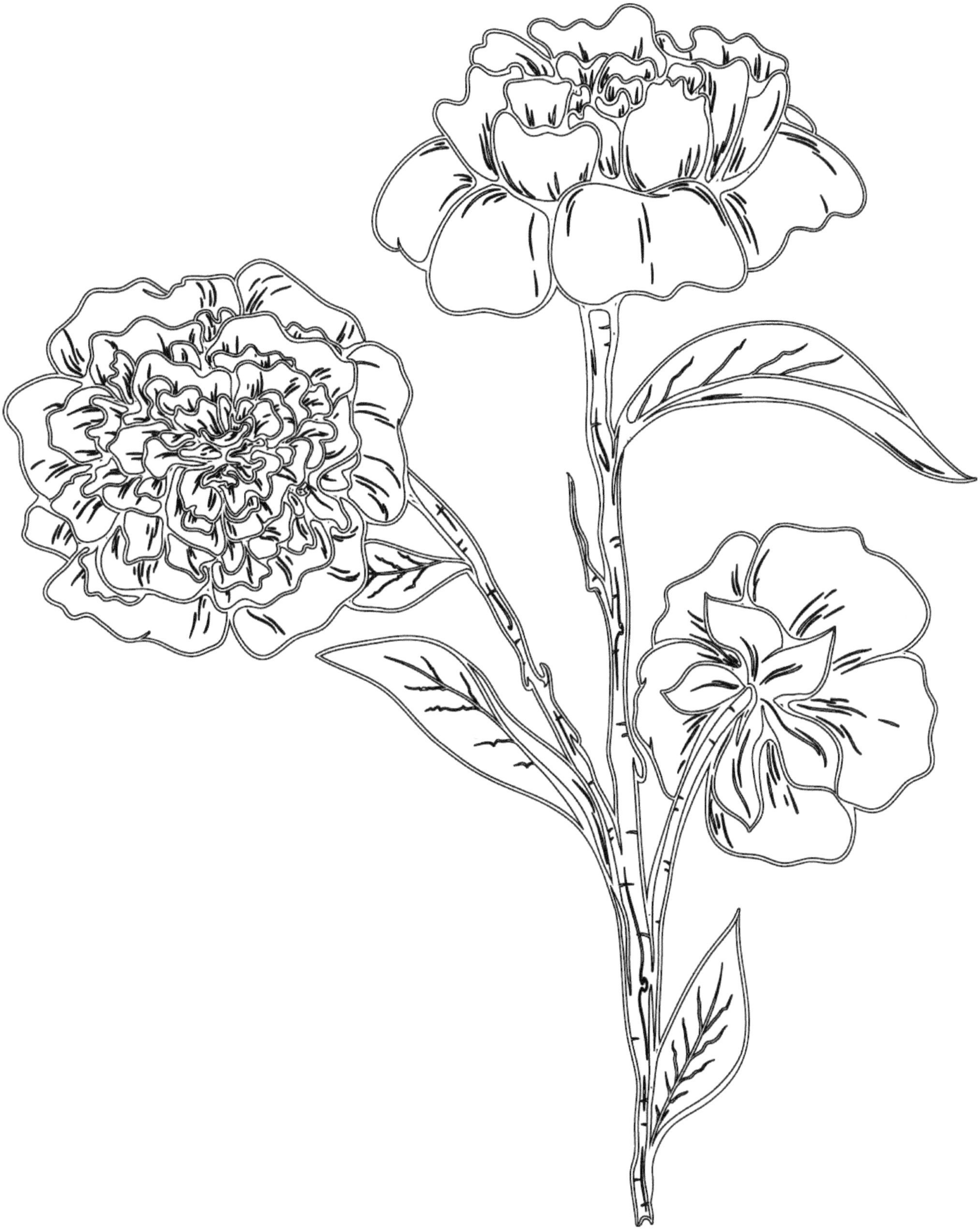

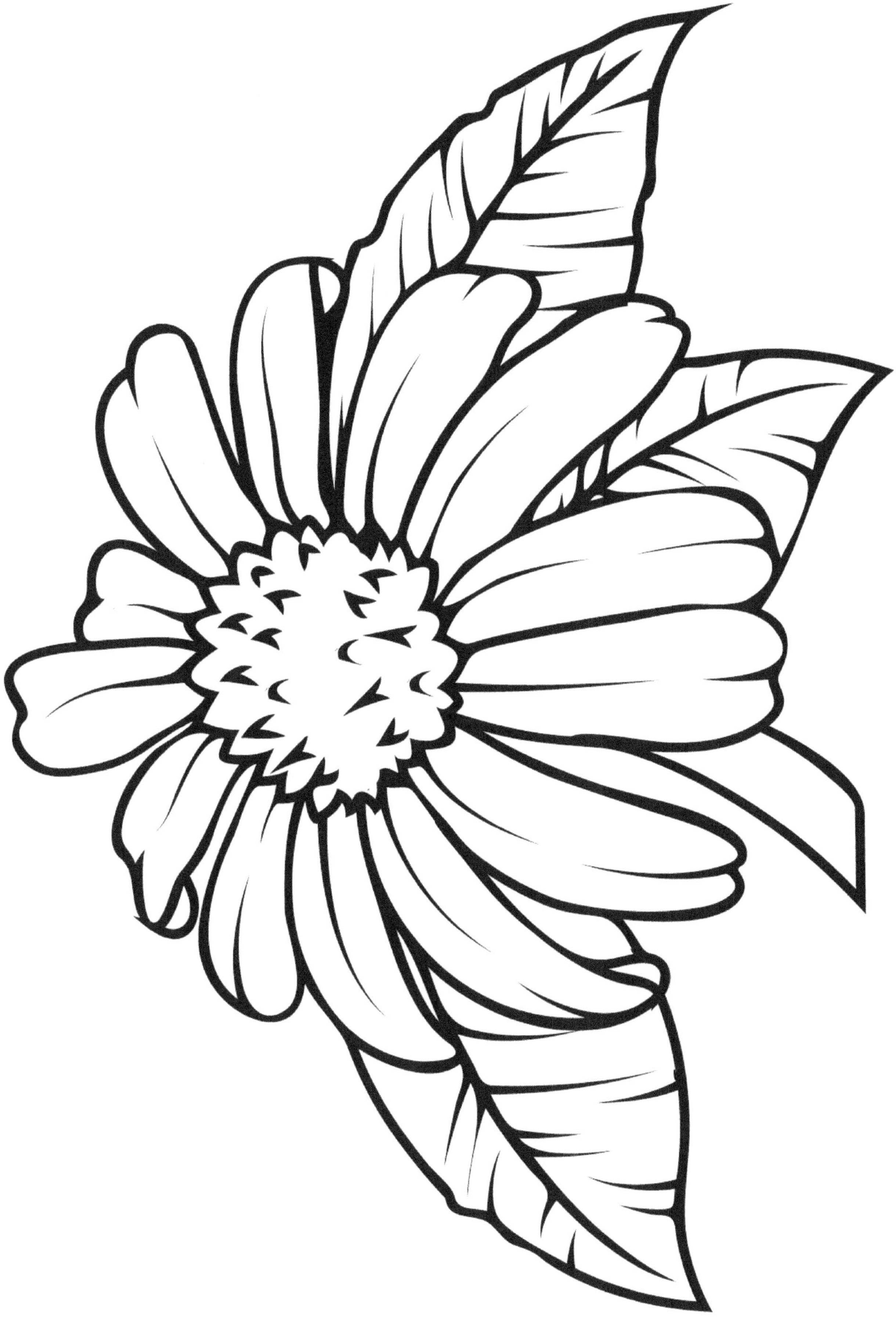

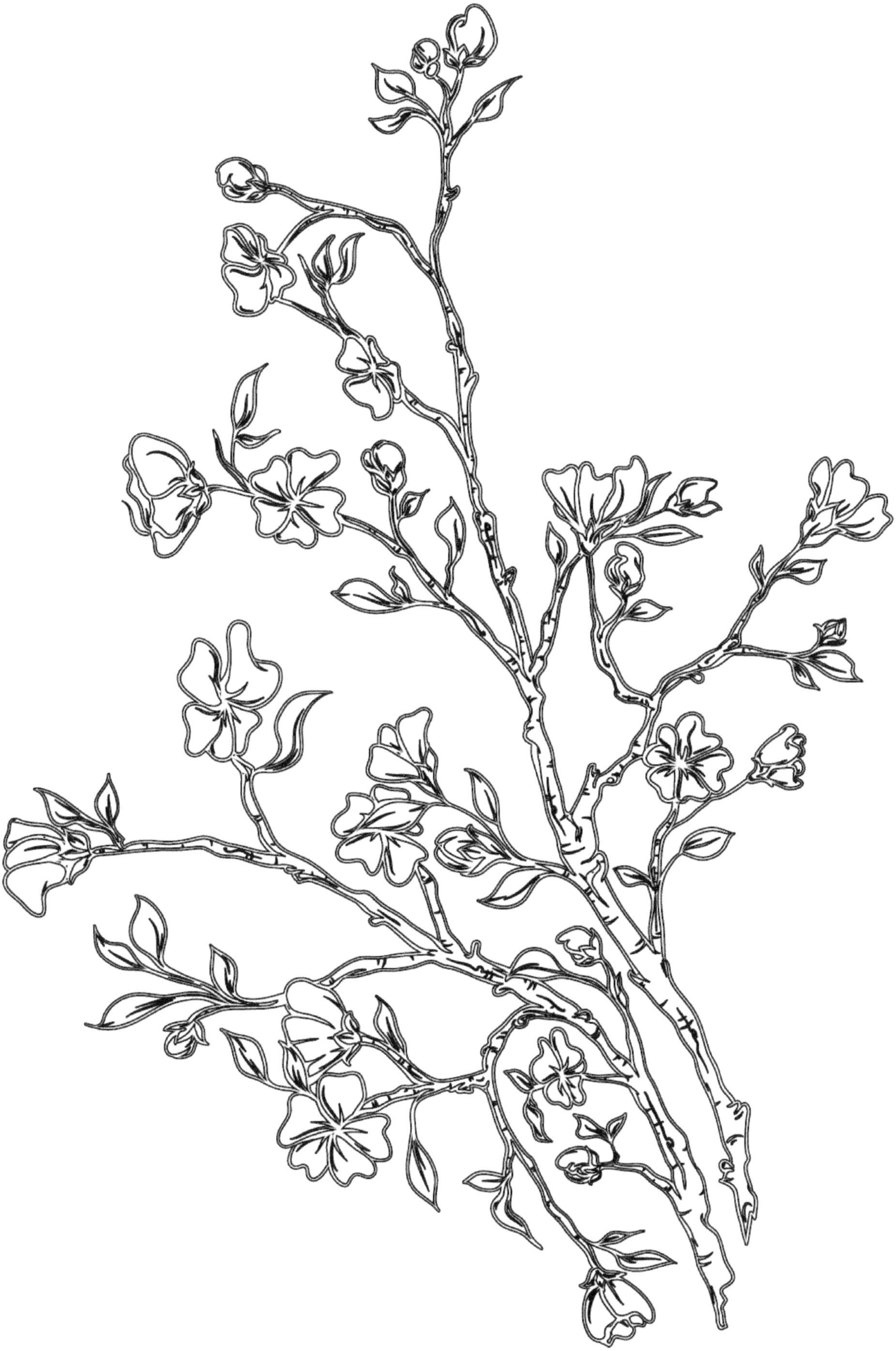

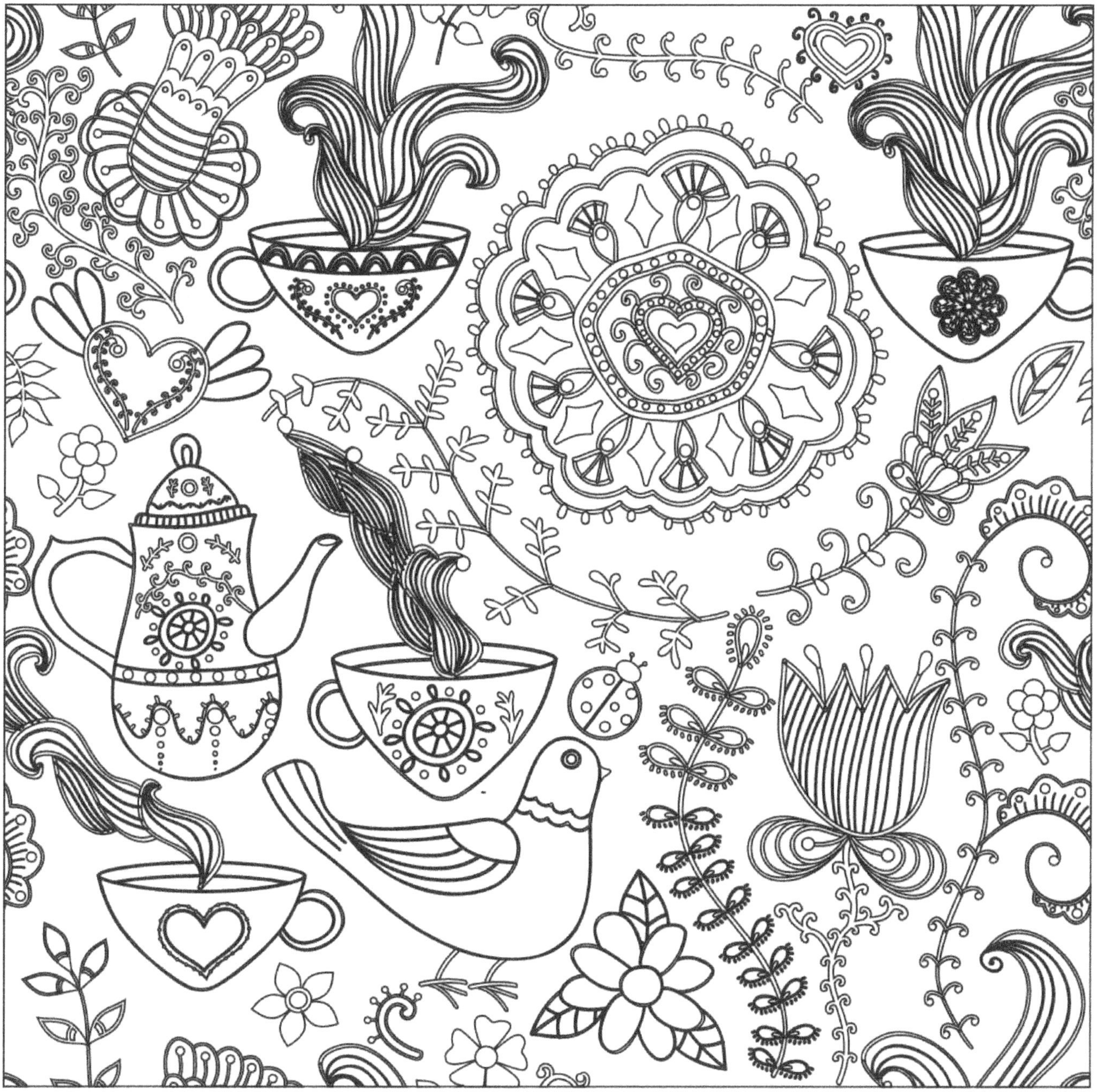

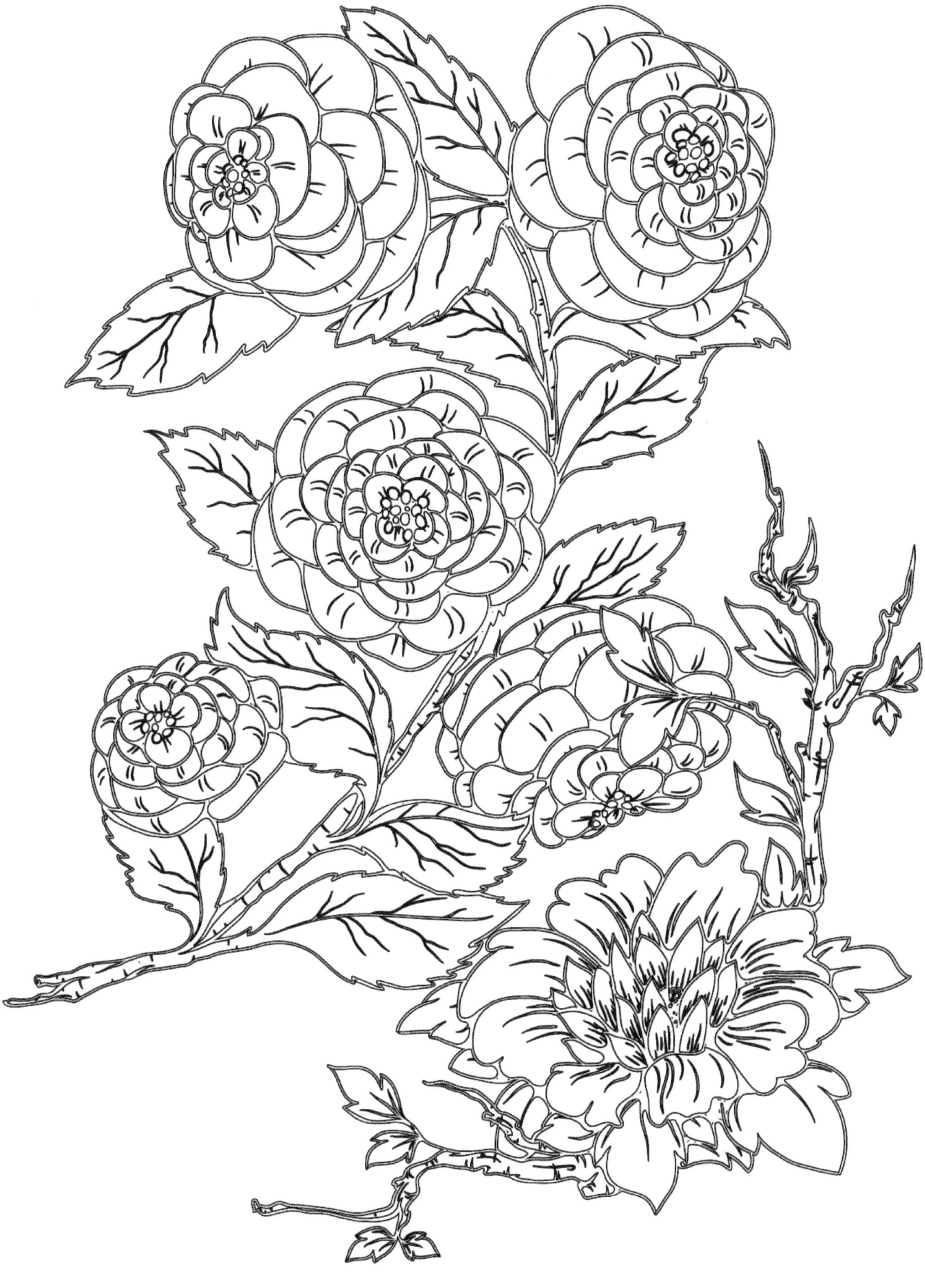

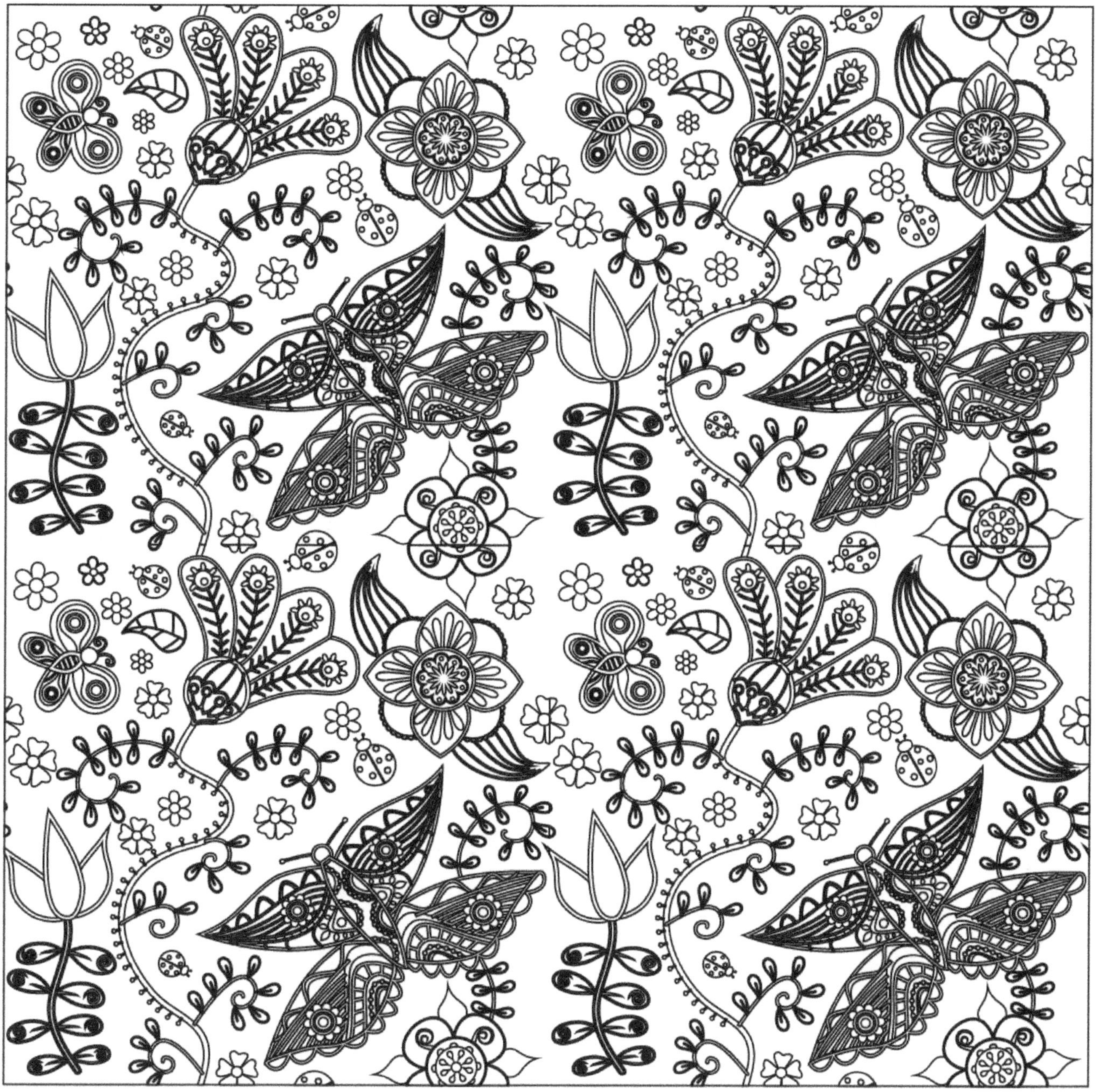

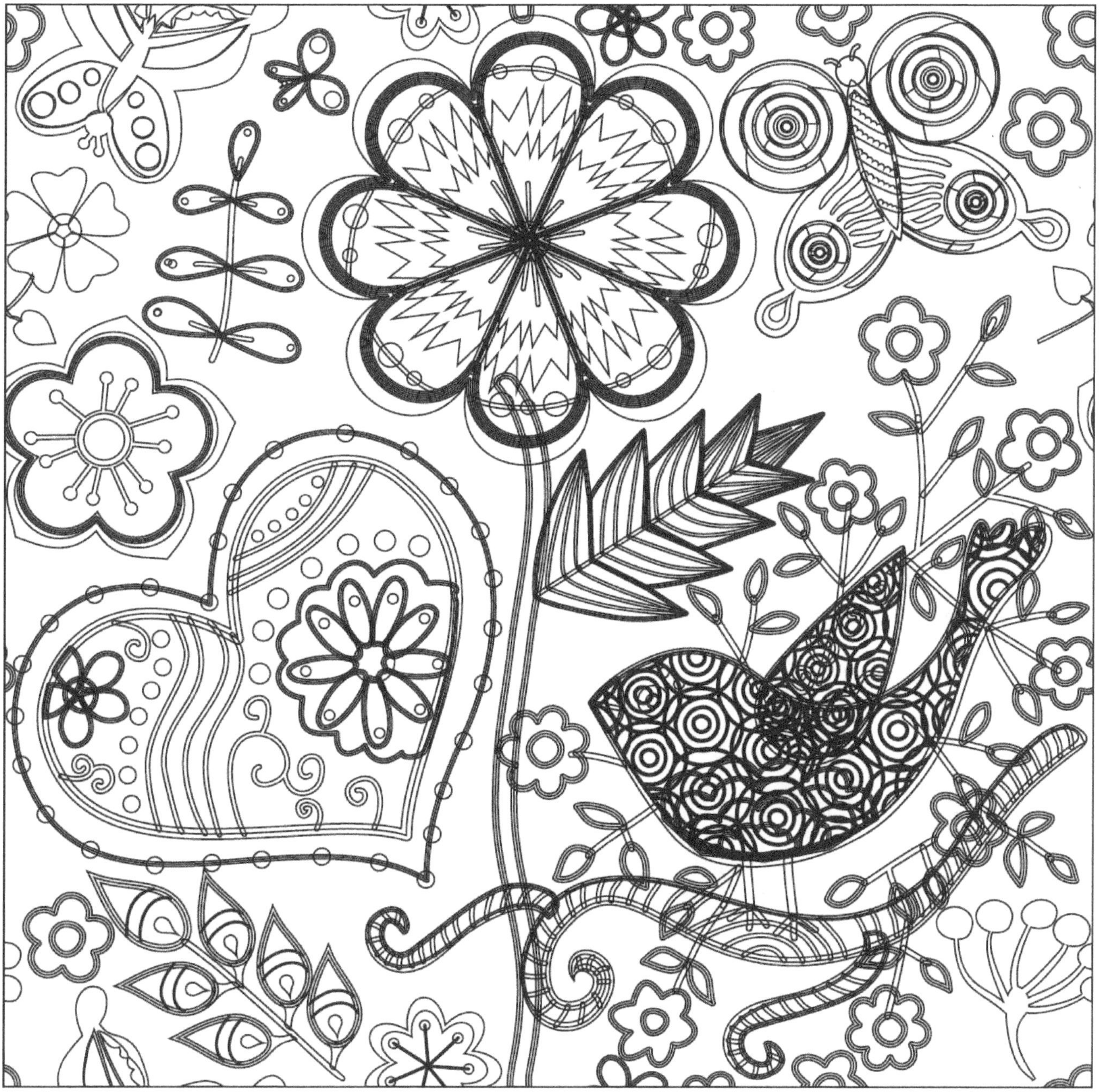

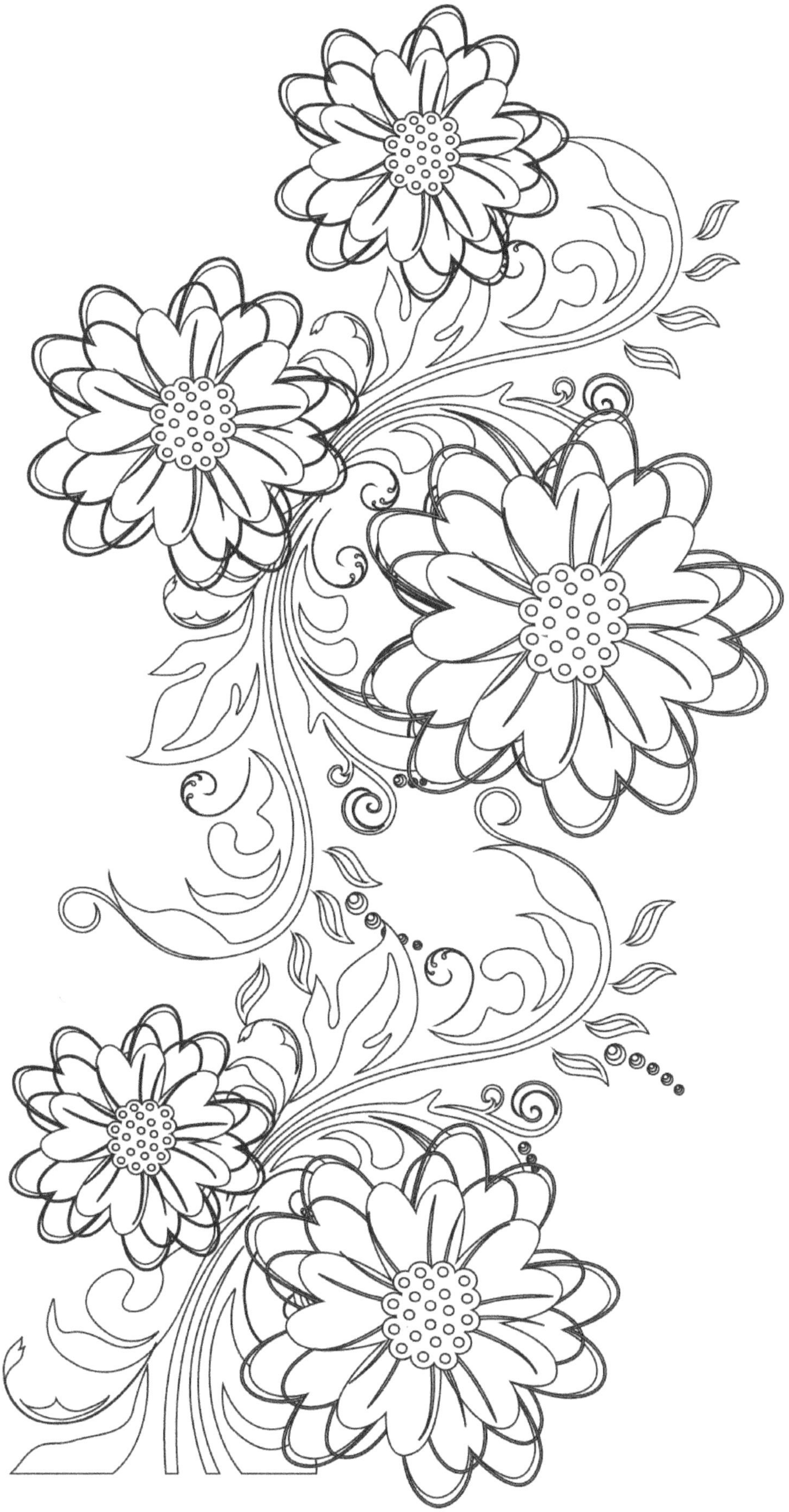

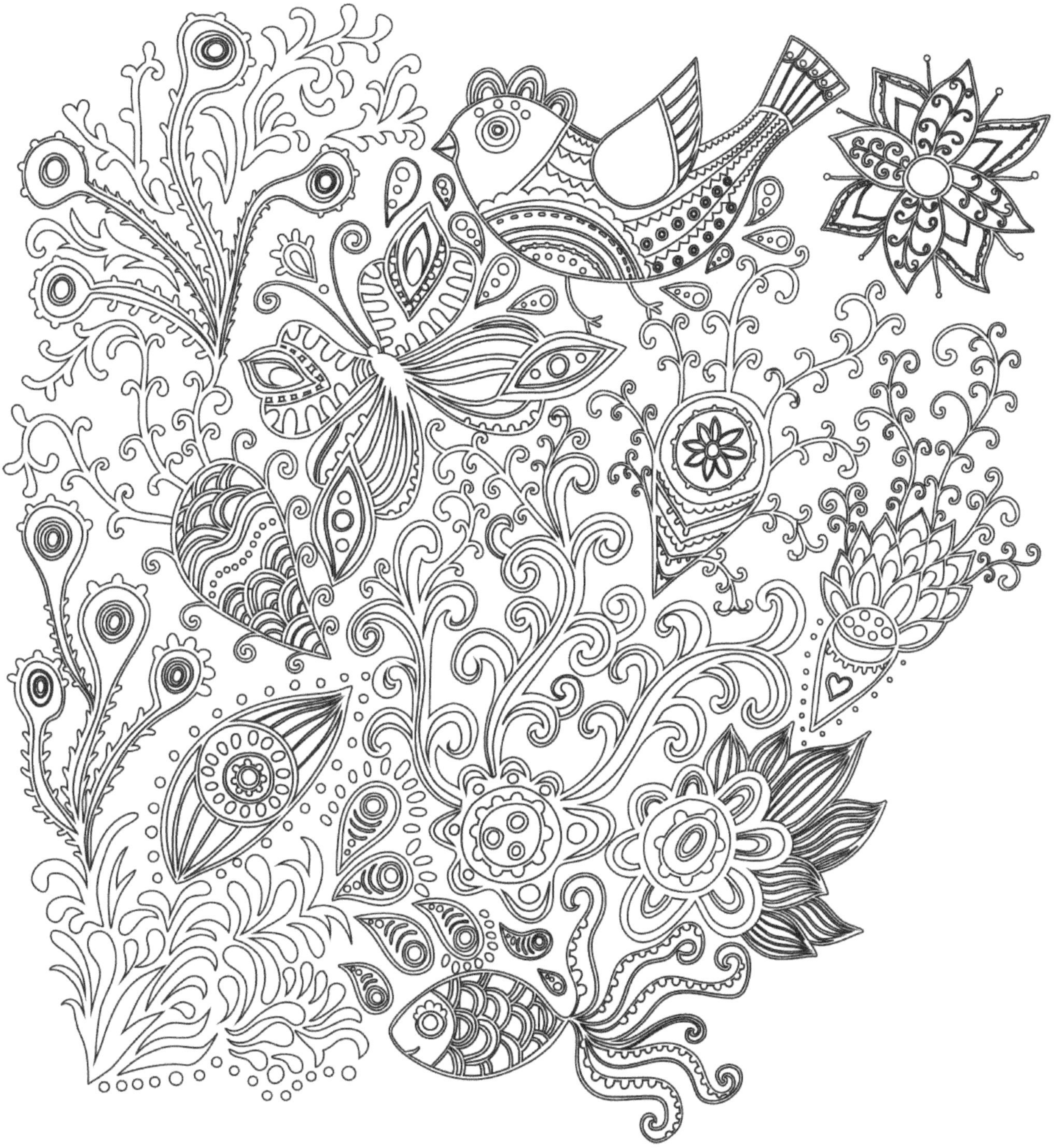

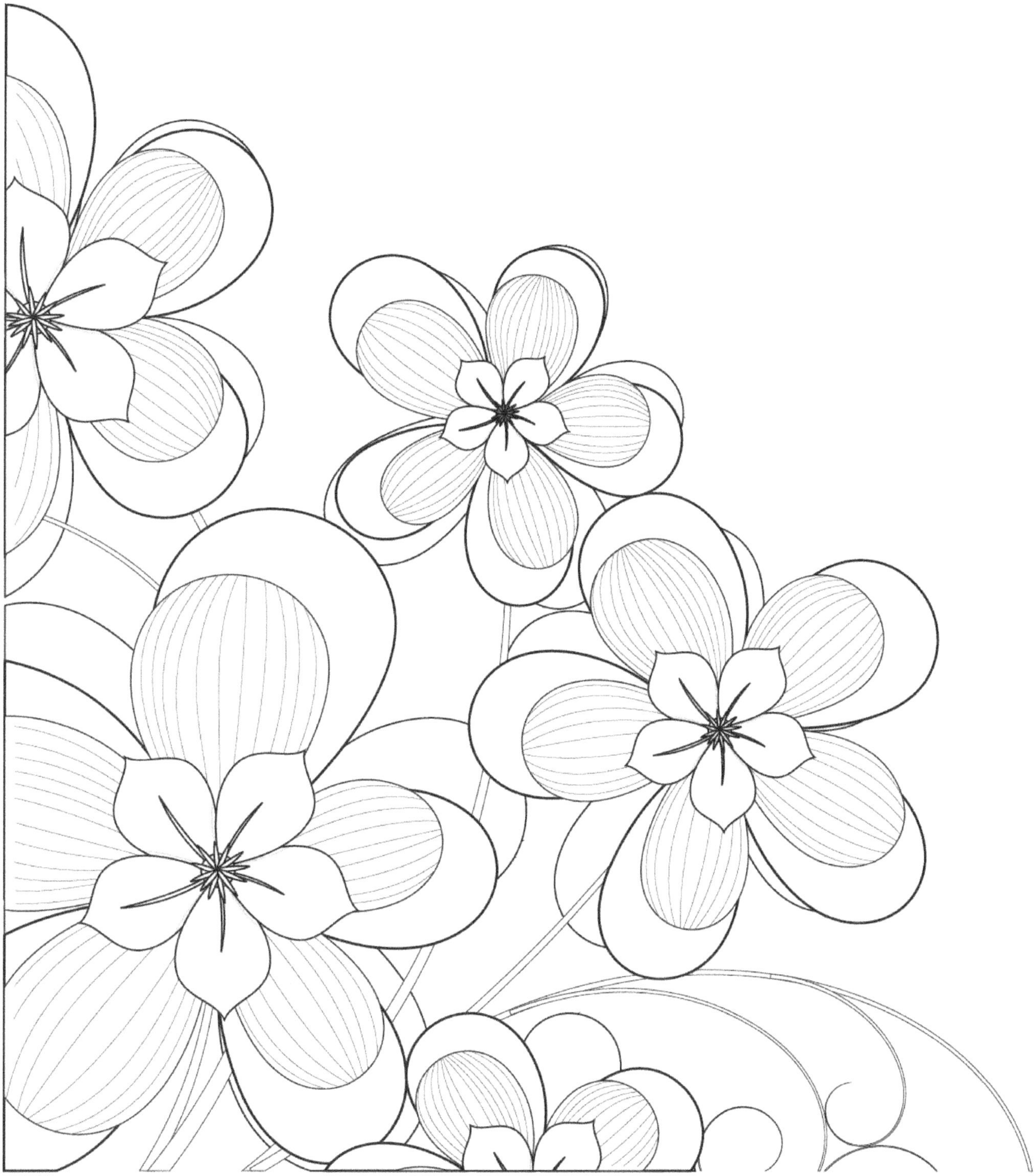

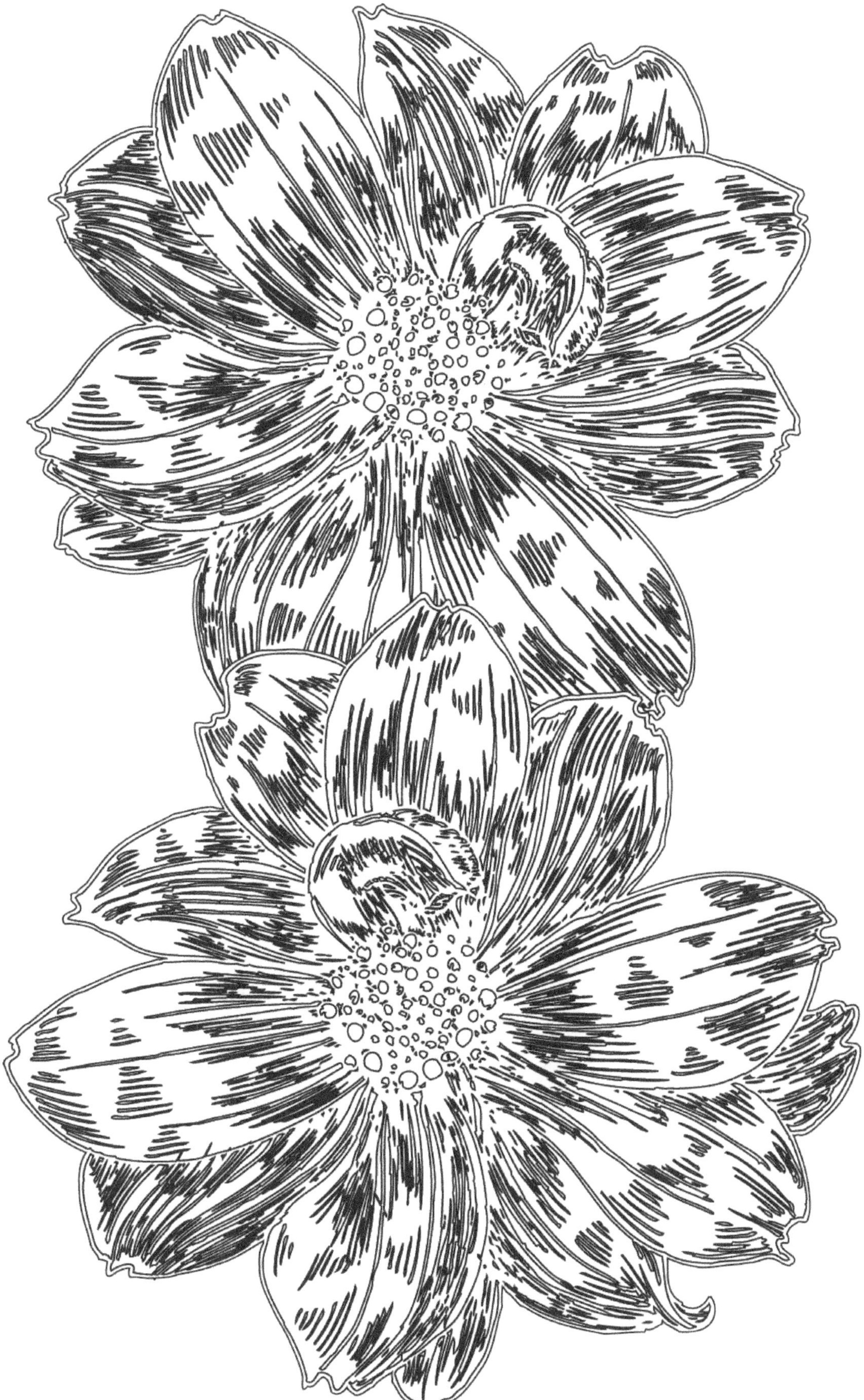

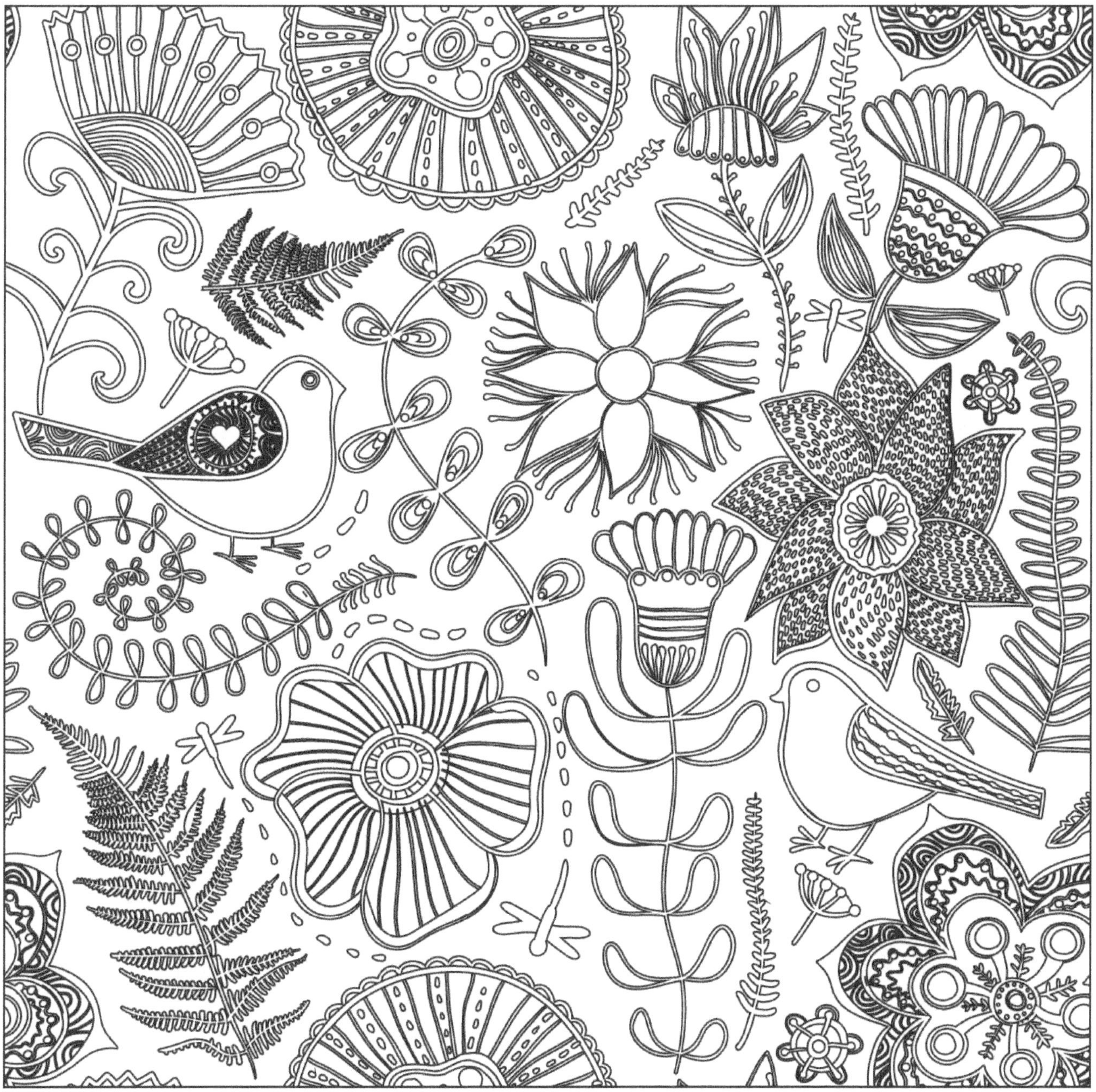

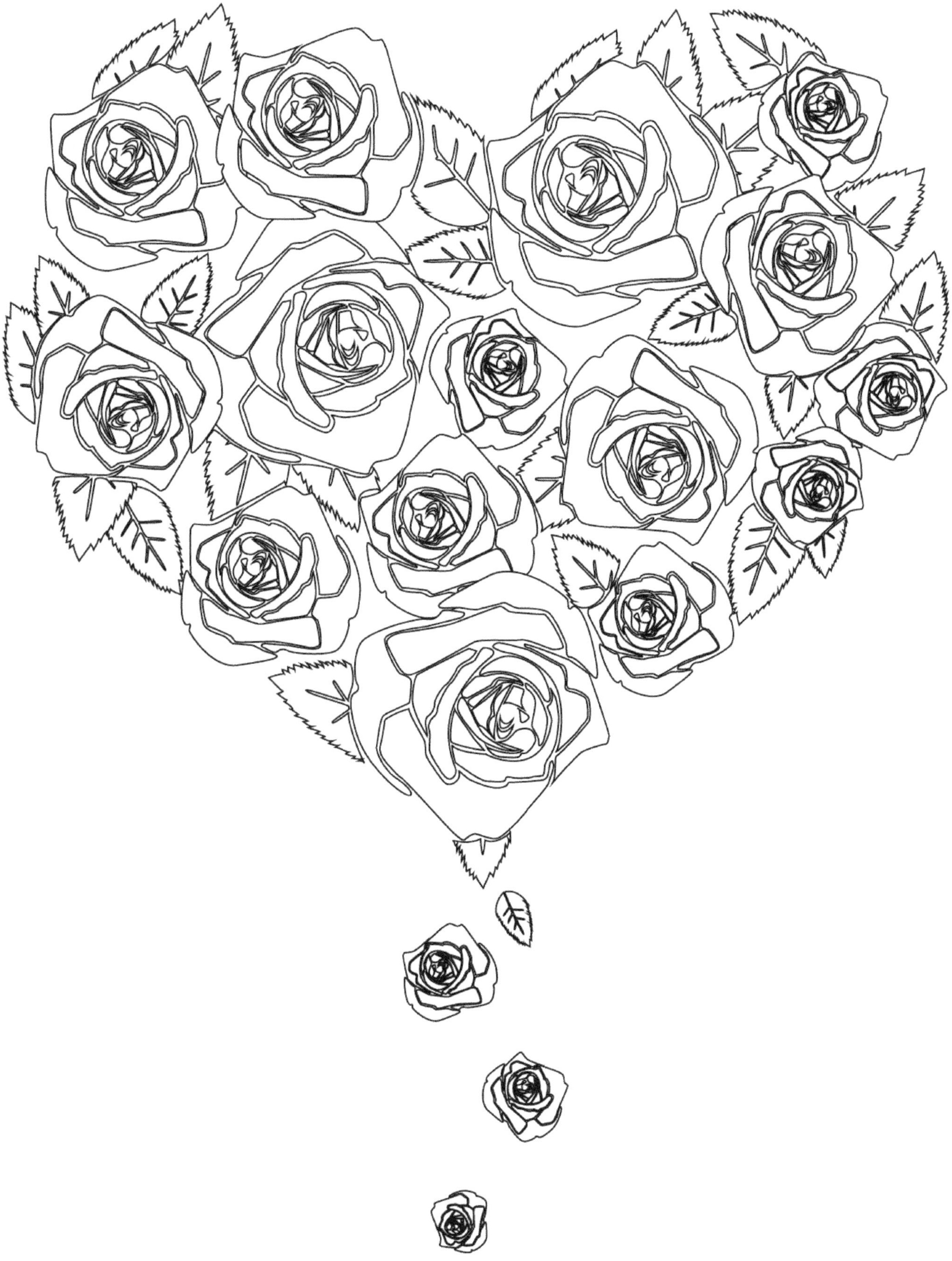

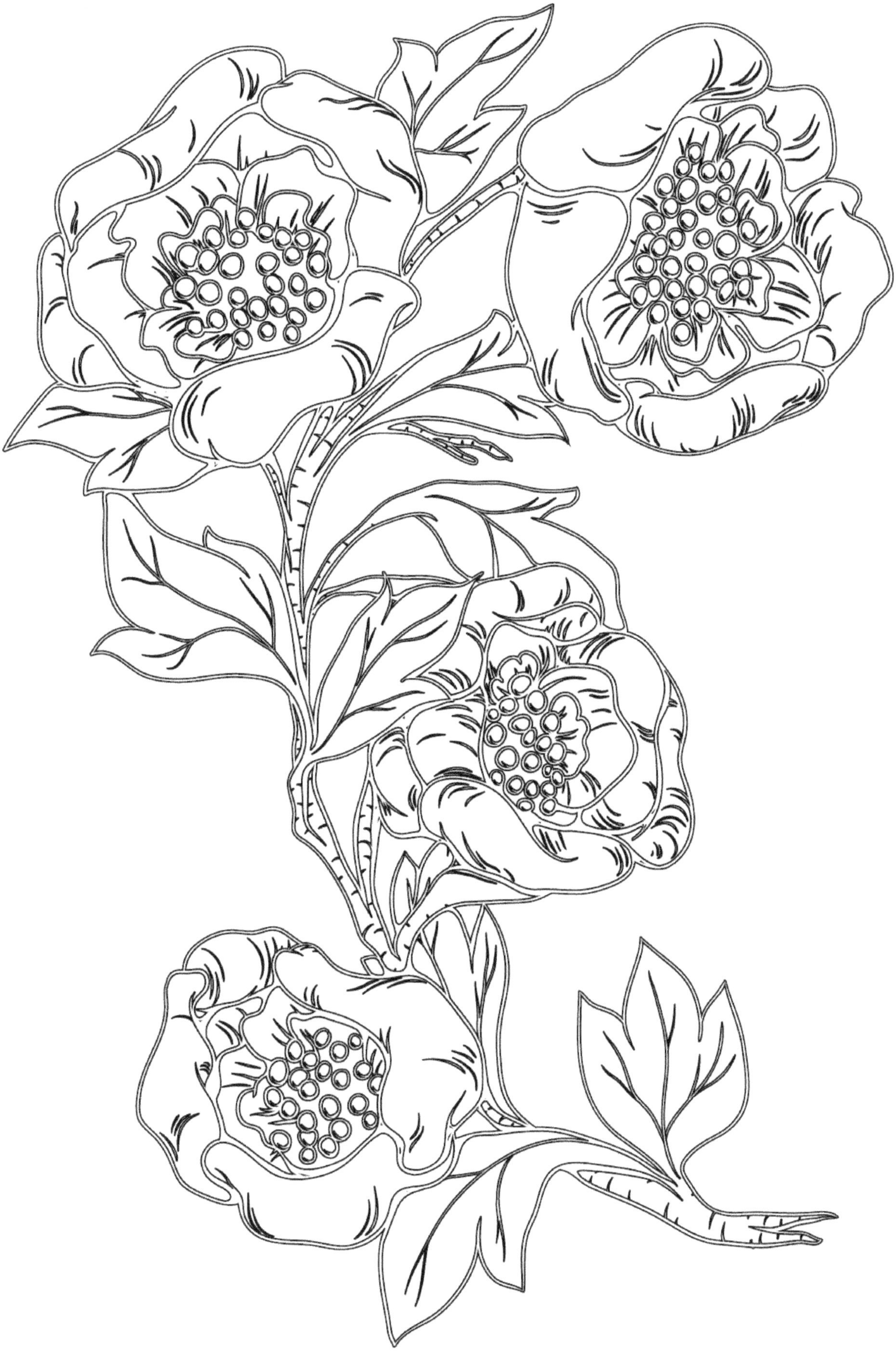

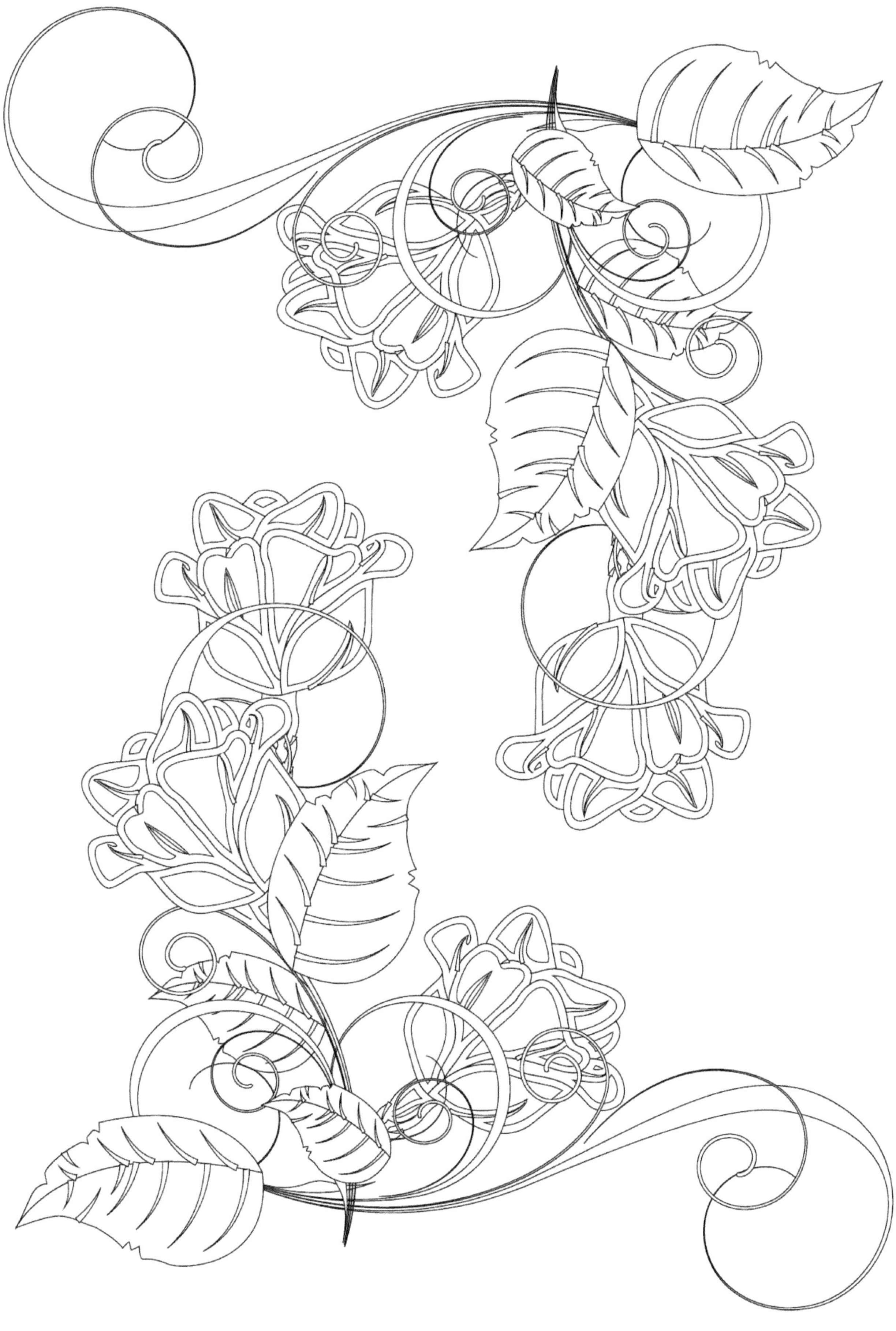

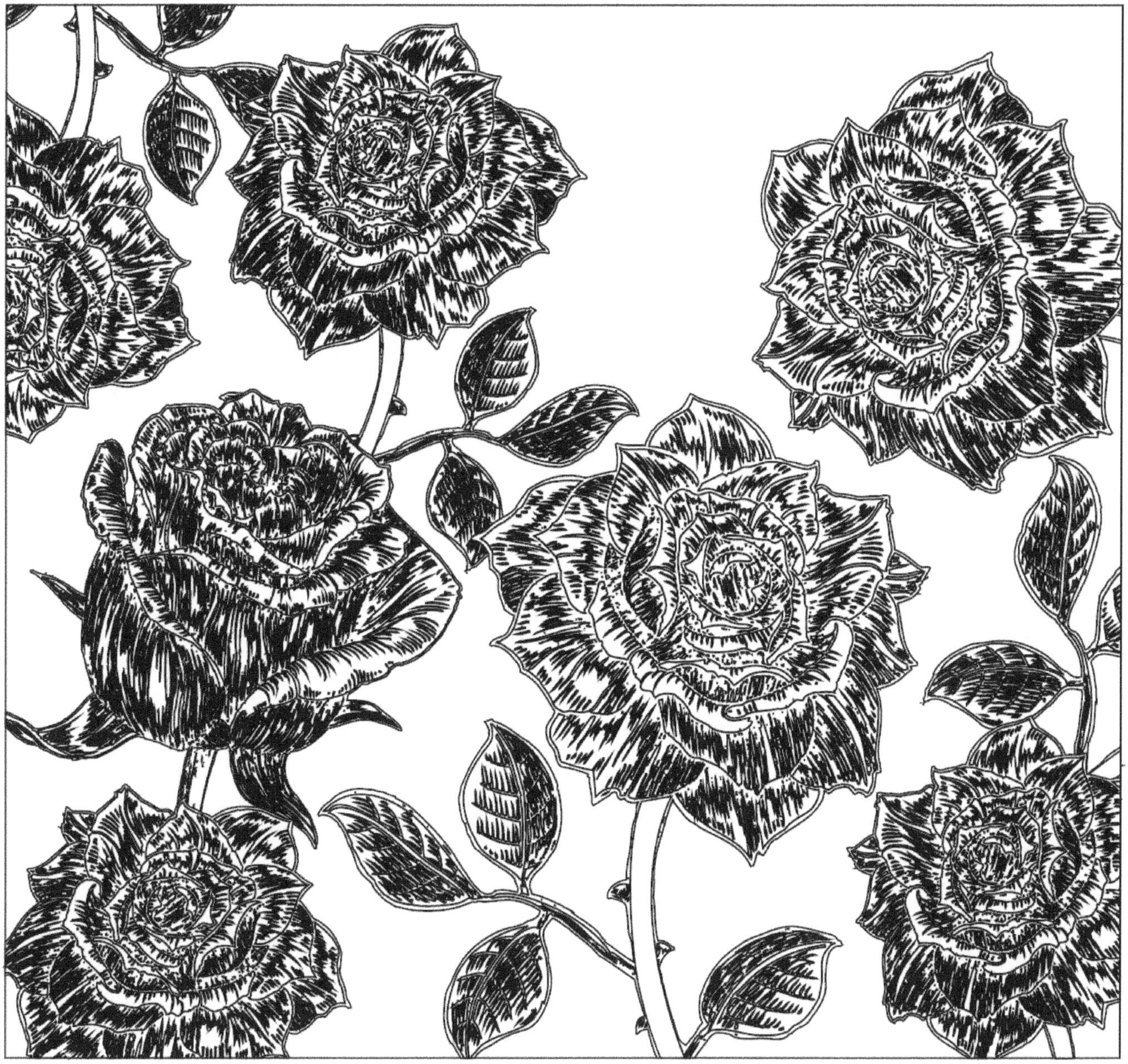

www.ingramcontent.com/pod-product-compliance
Lightning Source LLC
Chambersburg PA
CBHW080602190526
45169CB00007B/2854
* 9 7 8 1 5 3 5 2 4 5 6 3 0 *